CONTENTS

WORLD MACHINE

⌄ FOSSIL FUEL – a fuel, such as coal or natural gas, that is obtained from fossilized remains in the Earth

The Earth is not a dead rock. It is like a complicated, gigantic machine. Every machine needs power to work and the Earth gets all it needs from the Sun. The Sun drives the planet's climate, its winds and waves, and beneath the Earth's surface is a molten core – another source of heat and power. Much of today's technology is in some way linked to these basic resources.

Offshore turbines convert wind energy into electrical power.

Rigs out at sea are used to extract oil and gas fuel from beneath the ocean.

Water technology

The ocean covers about one-third of the planet, so making use of its potential is vital. Water and waves can be used to drive generators, as a way of producing electrical power without polluting the atmosphere.

wave farm off the coast of Portugal (*see page 18*)

Water drives electricity generators at hydroelectric power stations.

Geothermal power

Heat stored under the ground can be tapped to make power. In some places there are natural springs of hot water, but usually a hole is drilled down to hot rock. Water is pumped down the hole. This turns to steam, which shoots up to power a turbine and generator. Geothermal power stations do not need any fuel, nor do they produce any harmful gases.

geothermal power station in New Zealand

"The world, like any other machine, doesn't need a spanner in the works."

Fred Hoyle (1915–2001)
British astronomer

geothermal power plant

Engineering technology

Amazing bridges, tunnels and vehicles enable people to travel from place to place more quickly than ever, while satellites in space help us to find our way around the planet.

GPS (Global Positioning System) satellites circle the Earth (see page 28).

● NEW MATERIALS

In the 21st century, scientists are creating materials that do not occur in nature. These are composites (mixtures) made of different elements, designed to be very strong and light. Carbon nanotubes are the strongest material yet known. Lighter than hair, they are tougher than a diamond.

atoms in a chain reaction (see page 20)

Particle technology

The tiniest of particles can be used to propel a spacecraft through space, or split to release energy that can be converted into huge amounts of electrical power.

computer-generated artwork of a carbon nanotube (see pages 16 and 36)

Solar farms capture the power of the Sun (see page 24).

a game character, created and animated by computer software (see page 40)

a solar sail (see page 26)

Solar technology

The Sun's energy can be harnessed to power cars, planes, spacecraft and other vehicles. To help reduce our use of fossil fuels, which will one day run out, it is also used to heat homes and provide electricity.

Digital technology

Technology can also be fun. Advances in digital gaming and the internet mean that we can now play games with people living on the other side of the planet.

Conveyor belts

The small chips of rock are carried away on a conveyor belt powered by electric motors. If the belt is not near enough to the tunnel entrance it transfers the debris to railway trucks, which haul it away.

Tunnel segments

The tunnels are lined to prevent pieces of rock breaking off or, in softer ground, to stop the tunnel collapsing. The lining is made of concrete segments, which fit together to form a ring. The segments are pushed into place with pneumatic rams.

There are usually five to eight segments in each ring, plus a smaller 'key' piece.

MEGA -TUNNEL

Tunnels are very expensive to build, but they greatly speed up journeys by reducing the distance a vehicle has to travel from place to place. There are thousands of kilometres of tunnels in the world, through mountains, under rivers and even beneath the sea. These days most are created by huge tunnel boring machines (TBMs). TBMs make tunnelling faster and safer than in the days when miners had only shovels, drills and explosives.

Pneumatic jacks

Powerful pneumatic jacks, or rams, press against the side walls to change the direction of tunnelling. Other jacks push against the last ring of segments to propel the TBM forwards.

> The Rock of Gibraltar, off southern Spain, is like a honeycomb – 60km of tunnels have been dug there.

A mechanical worm

In nature, a shipworm bores through wood, which then passes through its body. A TBM is a mechanical version of this sea creature. It is a metal tube full of machinery, weighing thousands of tonnes. At the front, a rotating disc cuts into the rock, which is passed through the disc and back through the machine on a conveyor belt. The tube reinforces the tunnel roof while a strong lining is fitted. Powerful pneumatic jacks push the machine forwards.

operators in the control cabin

Alpine tunnel

The new Gotthard railway tunnel in Switzerland (shown in yellow) is much straighter and deeper than the older, more winding route it is replacing (shown in red). It will make the journey between Italy and Switzerland, through the Alps, much shorter and quicker.

When it is finished, in 2016, the 57km Gotthard Base Tunnel will be the longest in the world.

Switzerland

Italy

Cutting disc

The cutterhead acts like an enormous cheese grater, scraping off the rock using rows of cutting discs made from very tough steel. The discs quickly wear down and have to be changed. In very hard rock this might be as

Direction and speed

An operator drives and steers the TBM. Laser beams make sure it is always heading on the correct path. The average speed of a TBM, depending on the type of rock, is about 70cm

HYDRAULIC – operated by the pressurized movement of water, or other fluid, carried through pipes

Inside each pier is a staircase for maintenance workers to use.

The piers rose at a rate of 4m per day.

Temporary pier

When the concrete piers were finished, the steel decks for carrying the road were pushed out from either side of the valley. Temporary steel piers were built between the concrete ones to reduce the distance over which the decking had to be supported.

Concrete pier

Seven giant, reinforced concrete piers rise from the valley to carry the road. Pier Two is the tallest concrete pier in the world, at 245m above the ground. All seven have a combined height of 1.12km.

Hydraulic jacks or pistons pushed the temporary tower up 1m at a time.

Roadway across the gorge is 2.46km long.

Temporary piers were taken down once the steel decks were in place.

SUPERBRIDGE

Up until 200 years ago, bridges were made only of stone, brick and wood, which limited their size. The use of iron and steel, from the 19th century, made bigger bridges possible. Today, lightweight steel and other extra-strong materials allow engineers to build simply enormous bridges, capable of spanning seas as well as rivers and valleys. The Millau Viaduct in France (above) is an impressive example. There are even plans to bridge the Straits of Gibraltar so that people can drive directly from Europe to Africa.

The Millau Viaduct

This awe-inspiring structure spans the deep, wide gorge of the River Tarn in southern France, allowing a motorway to reach the Mediterranean. It is the tallest bridge ever built. It took ten years to plan and just over three to construct. The bridge was opened in December 2004. It cost 300 million euros (about £270 million) and, thankfully, not a single human life.

> The tallest mast top along the Millau Viaduct is 343m above the river – higher than the top of the Eiffel Tower in Paris, France.

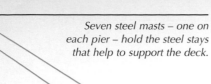

Seven steel masts – one on each pier – hold the steel stays that help to support the deck.

Screen protects the traffic from the 150km/h winds.

Deck is shaped like an upside-down aeroplane wing – so that the wind safely presses it down instead of lifting it up.

Steel decking

The road deck is made of steel rather than concrete. This makes the bridge lighter, slimmer and safer in high winds. But it still weighs 36,000 tonnes, excluding the weight of the tarmac on the road itself.

Each mast is 87m tall and weighs 700 tonnes.

Every stay is made up of 91 cables, which are each made from seven strands of steel.

⊖ MOVING THE DECKS INTO PLACE

A system of hydraulic jacks and wedges can be used to shift steel decks into place, 3cm at a time. Firstly, a lifting wedge is pushed out. This moves the pushing wedge and deck upwards. Secondly, a cylinder or jack moves the pushing wedge and deck forwards. Thirdly, the lifting wedge is pulled back again and the pushing wedge and deck are dropped. Lastly, the pushing wedge is moved back to its original position to repeat the first pushing action.

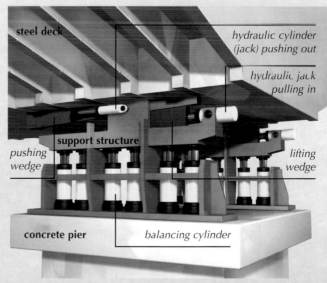

steel deck

hydraulic cylinder (jack) pushing out

hydraulic jack pulling in

support structure

pushing wedge

lifting wedge

concrete pier

balancing cylinder

ENGINE ROOM

▽ BOGIE – the swivelling undercarriage of a locomotive or carriage, with two or more pairs of wheels

For a journey of less than 500km, the electric train is quicker than a plane or a car and also produces fewer greenhouse gases. It is quieter than a plane and the track takes up less room than an airport or motorway. In 1960, Japan stunned the world by building a new line between Osaka and Tokyo, with electric trains speeding at an amazing 220km/h. The French railways went one better in the 1980s – their high-speed TGV trains can travel in excess of 300km/h.

The motor bogie

Six 'motor bogies' power a TGV train: three at each end. Each has two 1,000-horsepower electric motors connected to the axle, through gears. Each bogie is as powerful as a steam express engine, but weighs only as much as a small car.

"It's a pretty toy, but I don't see any use for it."

Michael Faraday (1791–1867)
British scientist, commenting on the world's first electric motor

traction motor

drive shaft

axle

output gear

motor gear

intermediate gear

crashproof driver's cab, with strong, anti-collision bulkhead

headlights and warning lights

front power car of a high-speed TGV (*Train à Grande Vitesse*)

automatic couplers for joining two TGVs together to run as one

03

TGV power

TGV trains do not need to carry fuel or large engines. Each one has 12 motors providing a grand total of 12,000 horsepower. This gives very high speed and also fantastic acceleration – any time lost is soon made up. In 2007, a TGV set a new world rail speed record of 575km/h.

> Ten countries already operate high-speed train services, and three more are either planning or building their own.

⊖ IN DEVELOPMENT: THE AGV

Technicians are developing a new version of the TGV, without the power cars at each end. In an AGV, all the electrical equipment is located under the floor and the motors are spread out along the train, in bogies between the carriages. With no power cars, it is 30 per cent lighter than the TGV and has more room for passengers. More power is transmitted directly to the wheels – so the AGV runs even faster while using less energy.

AGV front carriage under construction (left), and its sleek and comfortable driver's cab (above)

www.mos.org/sln/Leonardo/InventorsToolbox.html

All railway signals are shown on a display inside the cab.

Ventilating grilles prevent the power car from overheating.

circuit breakers and control equipment

The power car

The front carriage has equipment to convert and control energy from the overhead power line. The transformer receives 25,000 volts of electricity and reduces it to 1,500 volts for the motors. A computer makes sure the wheels turn at the right speed, so no power is wasted.

Copper power lines transmit the electric current.

Pantograph is a frame that collects the electric current.

main transformer

railway sleeper

Track curves are very gentle, with gravel ballast under the sleepers, to give a smooth, safe and speedy ride.

ROCKET SCIENCE

"We'll never be a great civilization as long as rain showers can delay the launch of a space rocket."

George Carlin (1937–2008)
American actor, author and stand-up comedian

To get a spacecraft into space, you need powerful rocket engines that can propel it upwards at 40,000km/h, the speed required to blast free of the Earth's gravitational pull. But once the craft is in space, there is virtually no gravity and none of the friction forces created by moving through the Earth's atmosphere, so very little power is needed to accelerate or change direction. This means a different type of engine can operate in space, using a lighter, more economical fuel.

ION – *an atom, or group of atoms, that has become electrically charged*

The fairing or nose cone protects the cargo as Soyuz climbs through the atmosphere.

Fregat's engine fires to steer the spacecraft into its final position.

Rocket stage separation

The rocket is built in 'stages'. Each stage fires its engines until its fuel is all burnt up. Then the next stage takes over. The four booster rockets provide most of the power at lift-off. They burn for about two minutes and then break away.

Fregat *is a controllable craft used to push the payload (cargo) into its correct orbit.*

Stage 3 is 6.7m long and weighs 23 tonnes.

Stage 2 is 28m long and weighs 102 tonnes.

First stage separation: the four boosters peel off and fall back to Earth.

Soyuz-Fregat

This type of rocket (left) is used to launch satellites and spacecraft into orbit from its launch site in Russia. It stands 42.5m tall and weighs 300 tonnes – all except 26 tonnes of that huge mass is made up of its liquid oxygen and kerosene fuel. More than 1,735 *Soyuz* rockets have been launched since 1966.

Four booster rockets make up Stage 1. Each one is 19.8m long and weighs 42 tonnes.

Second stage separation: the central core drops away and burns up as it hits the atmosphere.

> Of all the 300-plus tonnes that blast into space, as part of a *Soyuz* launch, only the 5-tonne payload remains in space.

The *BepiColombo* spacecraft will be launched in 2015, and is scheduled to reach Mercury in 2022.

Communication dish to receive commands and send back information.

Soyuz can carry a payload of 5.3 tonnes into space.

The rocket payload

The nose cone of *Soyuz* opens up and is discarded before the engine on the *Fregat* craft fires up. *Fregat*'s engine can be turned on and off to manoeuvre the payload into its final position. Then, the payload separates.

The ion engine's gas fuel is very light, so a large store of it can be carried on board – enough for missions lasting years.

Solar panels, once unfolded, will provide the electricity to charge the xenon gas and make the ion engine work

Ion thrusters

A long-distance spacecraft needs an engine that uses very little and very light fuel – otherwise it would be too heavy for a rocket to carry into orbit. So some spacecraft have an ion engine, which is fuelled by particles of xenon gas.

☉ THE ION ENGINE

An ion engine emits a high-speed stream of xenon gas particles from a nozzle. These particles push the spacecraft forwards. The thrust is very gentle – about the same as a piece of paper pressing on your hand. But, as there is no resistance in space, this is enough – over time – to propel the craft to speeds of more than 16,000km/h.

Electricity is used to charge the atoms inside the chamber, so that they become ions.

ionization chamber

The charged ions are channelled into a beam.

The beam of ions creates thrust, which pushes the spacecraft in the opposite direction.

supply of xenon atoms

∨ GLIDING – Flying without any power: for a plane, the forward motion keeps air flowing over the wings to keep it aloft

Left WK2 cabin is used to view SS2 launch; one on right is for SS2 training.

SpaceShipTwo (SS2) passenger spacecraft

wingspan of 43m

The mother ship is called WhiteKnightTwo (WK2).

PW 308A jet engine

Zero-G experience

When there is no gravity, there is no up or down, so the cabin has viewing windows on its roof, sides and floor. Handholds on the sides of the cabin allow the passengers to move about.

V GALACTIC

emergency exit hatch   pilots' cabin

The passenger craft is known as SpaceShipTwo (SS2).

SPACE TOURS

A spacecraft has been designed to reach the edge of space, about 100km above Earth. It will not orbit (circle) the planet like a space station or satellite – but the crew and passengers will actually enter space for a few minutes, and experience weightlessness, before the craft returns to the ground. The two-and-a-half hour voyage will cost passengers about $200,000 (about £135,000), for five precious minutes of zero-gravity floating time.

Into orbit

The spaceship is carried up to a height of about 15km beneath the wings of a mother ship. This flies using four ordinary jet engines. When the passenger spacecraft is released, its rocket engine fires and blasts it up to an amazing 110km, at roughly 4,000km/h. The engine cuts out so that the craft coasts for the last few thousand metres, to hang in space for a few minutes.

> These vehicles (above) are based on the spacecraft designs that won a competition known as the X Prize, in 2004.

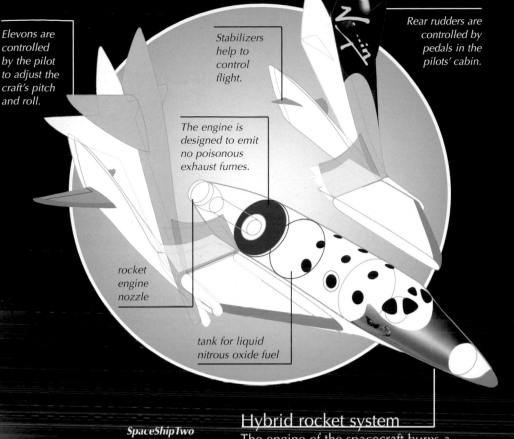

Elevons are controlled by the pilot to adjust the craft's pitch and roll.

Stabilizers help to control flight.

Rear rudders are controlled by pedals in the pilots' cabin.

The engine is designed to emit no poisonous exhaust fumes.

rocket engine nozzle

tank for liquid nitrous oxide fuel

SpaceShipTwo reaches a maximum height of 110km.

Hybrid rocket system

The engine of the spacecraft burns a mixture of liquid nitrous oxide and a solid rubber propellant to gain maximum power. It burns for only 90 seconds. Other than switching the engine on and off, the pilot has no control over it.

THE SPACEPORT

The flights will take off from Spaceport America at Upham, New Mexico, USA. The new terminal looks a little like a spacecraft itself – designed by Norman Foster, who also worked on the Millau Viaduct (*see pages 8–9*). To make it as ecologically friendly as possible, the spaceport is partly buried in the ground to keep it cool by day and warm at night.

For now, only one space flight from the port will be scheduled per day.

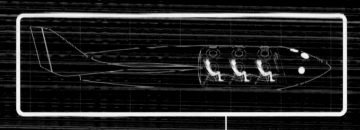

Return journey

When the rocket engine runs out of fuel, the rear wings lift up. This slows the spacecraft to 300km/h as it glides back to Earth. It re-enters the atmosphere at a much slower speed than other spacecraft, building up less friction, so it does not risk burning up during re-entry.

Passenger spacecraft

The spacecraft is as big as a medium-sized executive jet or a small bus. It has seats for two pilots and six passengers. The cabin was designed to allow the passengers to float around freely during their five minutes of weightlessness.

The spacecraft drops down to 23km – then the wings extend and it begins to glide.

The spacecraft slowly glides down to land at the spaceport.

Elevator car

Passengers and cargo will be carried inside an elevator car that will climb up the ribbon to a space station orbiting the planet. Unlike an ordinary lift, which is pulled up by cables, the space elevator will climb the ribbon with grips or rollers, a bit like a koala bear using its claws to climb up a tree. Photoelectric cells on the outside will convert a laser beam, beamed from below, into electrical power for the elevator car.

Passenger car will have to be pressurized, like the cabin of a spacecraft, so that those on board can breathe.

Carbon-based material is 20 times lighter than steel and 180 times as strong.

Carbon nanotubes

An extremely strong and light material will be needed to create a wire capable of supporting the space elevator. Carbon nanotubes could be the solution. Carbon is a very strong element and can be arranged to form tiny threads that are just one nanometre thick.

> NANOMETRE (NM) – *1nm is equal to a thousand-millionth (or a billionth) of a metre*

SPACELIFT

Rockets are a very expensive – and dangerous – way of carrying things into space. The journey would be much simpler if there was a tower or lift that people could use to climb into orbit.

A tower built of ordinary materials would be too heavy to stand upright. But scientists and engineers are working on a way to attach a wire to a satellite, orbiting the Earth, so that an elevator can travel up it. To achieve this the wire, or ribbon, would need to be attached to a counterweight (*see diagram, below*).

"The space elevator will be built about 50 years after everyone stops laughing."
Arthur C Clarke (1917–2008)
British science fiction author and inventor

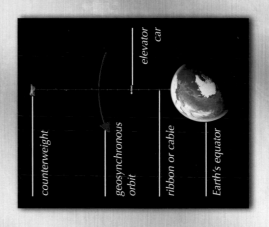

- counterweight
- elevator car
- geosynchronous orbit
- ribbon or cable
- Earth's equator

A DIRECT ROUTE INTO SPACE

The ribbon would extend from the Earth, 35.5km up to a station or satellite travelling on a 'geosynchronous' orbit. This means the station remains above the same spot as it goes around the Earth. Beyond the station, the ribbon would run out into space for nearly 100,000km with its end attached to a large weight – possibly a small, captured asteroid. As the counterweight goes around the Earth, it would pull the ribbon to keep it tightly stretched out.

A laser beam, focused by mirrors, provides electrical power for the elevator car as it travels into space.

Base station
The ribbon will be anchored on the Earth at a base station. Here, a power station will focus a laser beam up to the elevator as a source of electrical power. The base station will have to be on or very near the equator, where the Earth moves fastest. This will help to keep the ribbon pulled tight.

> For return journeys, the elevator car could be detached from the ribbon to fly down through the Earth's atmosphere like a space shuttle does.

The first-ever working wave farm, shown here, was moored off the coast of Portugal in 2006.

'Sea snake' generators

Sausage-shaped trains of steel cylinders are anchored to the sea floor, facing the direction of the waves as they roll into shore. Each one is 140m long and divided into three sections. As the waves move up and down, the sections bend at their hinged joints. The moving joints drive hydraulic motors inside, and this powers generators that make electricity.

Joints and hinges

The joints of the units are the most important parts. The cylinders in between are simply hollow tubes to keep the whole system afloat. Each joint has a hinge connecting it to a smaller cylinder that contains the power-generating equipment.

buoyancy cylinder

There are three generating units in each train of cylinders.

WAVE FARMING

The ocean is the greatest potential store of renewable energy in the world – and in recent years, scientists and engineers have developed new ways of harvesting the power of the waves. Water is 1,000 times more dense than air, so its potential energy is very much greater than that of the wind. Power generated from waves will never run out and can send no greenhouse gases into the atmosphere. It is the ultimate green – or 'blue' – fuel.

Junction boxes

The electric current produced by each unit is carried down cables to a junction box on the seabed. This connects the lines from all three generators to the main power cable that carries the electricity from the wave farm to the shore.

> Depending on how rough the sea is, each generator can provide electrical power for up to 500 homes.

hydraulic fluid (blue and pink)

electrical generator

hydraulic ram, or piston

pressure-equalizing equipment

hydraulic motor

Hydraulic pump and motor

This unit converts the wave motion into electricity. As the sections on either side move up and down on the waves, they push hydraulic rams backwards and forwards. The two rams always work in opposite directions, pumping fluid through a small hydraulic motor to turn an electrical generator.

001

"When I see a mighty wave beating the shore, I think of a great horse idly pawing the grass and long to set it in harness."

Sir George Sydenham Clarke (1848–1933)
British military engineer

cable from individual generator

main power line

mooring cable

⊖ HOW AN AQUABUOY WORKS

An 'aquabuoy' can also generate power from the waves. A long, open-ended steel tube hangs down from a floating buoy. As the waves move, the water pushes a piston up and down inside the tube. This forces water through a high-pressure pump to drive a turbine, which then turns a generator to make electricity.

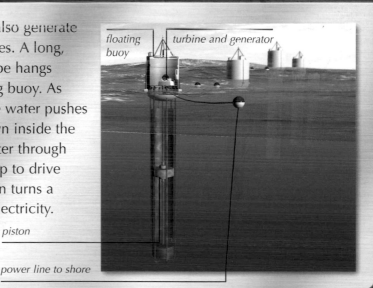

floating buoy

turbine and generator

piston

power line to shore

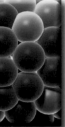

PARTICLE POWER

Nuclear power is one way of creating lots of energy without releasing harmful greenhouse gases into the atmosphere. Sadly, the process is expensive and potentially hazardous – the costs of safety are high and the dangerous waste products must be stored safely for many years while their radioactivity dies away. But for many, the power contained inside tiny atoms is the answer to our future energy needs.

NEUTRON – a particle with no electrical charge, which makes up an atom along with a proton and electrons

A nuclear plant

A nuclear power station consists of three basic units: the reactor that creates heat and steam, a turbine driven by the steam and a generator, powered by the turbine, that makes electricity. To make the process as safe as possible, all the machinery must be built to the highest standards. The risk of anything failing, exploding or leaking is kept as small as possible.

SPLITTING THE ATOM

1. A single neutron is fired into the unstable nucleus of an atom.

2. The nucleus splits into two. As it does so, it releases energy and some more neutrons.

3. The new neutrons shoot off to split more nuclei and release more energy and more neutrons. This is the chain reaction.

This splitting process (above) is known as nuclear fission.

All things are made up of tiny particles called atoms, and at the centre of every atom is a nucleus. When a nucleus is split, a tiny amount of the energy that holds the atom together is released. When billions of atoms are split, the energy created is enormous. This can be released as a controlled and constant supply of useful energy known as a chain reaction.

"Whoever talks about getting power on an industrial scale from splitting the atom is talking moonshine."

Ernest Rutherford (1871–1937)
scientist from New Zealand

> The energy in a lump of uranium the size of a sugar cube is enough to power a submarine across the Atlantic Ocean.

Cooling towers condense the steam from the turbine, turning it back into liquid water.

www.brainpop.com/science/energy/nuclearenergy/preview.weml

The turbine

High-pressure steam passes inside the turbine through the sets of blades and spins them around at extremely high speed. These turn a shaft, which is connected to the generator that produces the electricity.

Connection to the grid

Nuclear power stations are usually built in remote coastal areas, where there is a plentiful water supply. The electricity they produce is fed into the national grid and carried on high power lines to where it is needed.

uranium-fuelled reactor core

Strong steel casing resists the great heat and pressure inside.

control rods (red), made of boron

Graphite reactor core slows down the neutrons, causing more fission and getting more energy from the fuel.

Fuel cells of uranium oxide (purple) fit into these channels. Each cell lasts for several years.

The reactor

To produce a steady chain reaction, the reactor is controlled by rods made of boron. The rods absorb neutrons. When rods are lifted out of the core, fewer neutrons are absorbed and the reaction speeds up. When rods are lowered in, the reaction slows.

Water is pumped into the bottom of the reactor, to be heated and turned into steam.

NUCLEAR POWERED

A nuclear-powered submarine can stay deep and hidden underwater for as long as it needs to – without having to surface to recharge. It could stay submerged for years before the reactor needed refuelling, but this might damage the health of the crew on board. As long as the sailors remain physically and mentally fit, and have adequate supplies, there are few reasons to visit the surface.

BALLAST – *a heavy material put aboard a ship to make it stable in the water, or in a submarine to make it submerge (sink)*

Periscope and the radio, radar and direction-finding antennae are painted with irregular patterns to make them difficult to see.

Ohio class submarine

Each carrying 24 Trident nuclear missiles, the 18 submarines of the 'Ohio class' are the biggest in the mighty US Navy. Their nuclear-powered engine means that they can lie hidden in the seas for months at a time, always armed and ready to strike.

Fin or sail serves as a mounting for the periscopes and antennae, and as an observation platform when the submarine is surfaced.

Diving planes tilt up and down to increase the speed of diving, and to control depth when underwater.

Very strong inner pressure hull, 75mm thick, contains all the living quarters and machinery spaces.

Crew quarters

Each underwater mission lasts for about three months, so the 155 crew members are given very comfortable quarters, with good food and entertainment.

Sonar

A submarine 'sees' through its sonar (*sound navigation and ranging*) equipment. This sends out a noise that bounces back if it hits an object. Computers then work out the size, distance and direction of the object.

Sonar dome or boom, which emits pulses of sound, is located in the bow (front end) of the submarine.

The first submarine to be powered by a nuclear reactor was the *USS Nautilus*, launched in 1955.

Inside the reactor chamber

A small but very powerful nuclear reactor generates lots of heat. A circuit of water, under high pressure, passes through the reactor and is turned into steam. The steam drives a turbine, which powers the propeller and also a generator that makes electricity for the systems on board.

sealed reactor chamber

Rudder steers the submarine from side to side.

Propeller has seven blades, specially designed to make as little noise as possible.

Cycle of water

The steam is condensed – cooled and changed back into liquid water – and returned to the reactor vessel where it is reheated. This can go on for as long as the reactor remains active and the machinery does not wear out.

Drive shaft connects turbine to propeller.

ballast tank

High-pressure air is released from these bottles to force water out of the ballast tanks.

Stern (rear) diving planes adjust the depth and angle of diving.

"It navigates the watery deep all by itself: no storms to brave, because just a few metres beneath the waves, it finds absolute tranquillity!"

Jules Verne (1828–1905)
from his novel **Twenty Thousand Leagues Under The Sea**

⊖ DIVING AND SURFACING

To dive, water is taken into the submarine's ballast tanks. This makes it heavier so that it sinks. When the crew want to surface, compressed air forces the water out of the ballast tanks so that the submarine becomes light enough to float on the surface. An Ohio class submarine is 2,500 tonnes heavier, when submerged, than it is when it is surfaced.

submarine submerging, or diving

submarine emerging, or surfacing

SOLAR FARMING

"The Sun does not shine for a few trees and flowers, but the wide world's joy."

Henry Ward Beecher (1813–87)
American clergyman

Pure sunlight is the most renewable and unpolluting source of energy, so more and more is being done to try and harness it. One way of generating enormous heat is to magnify, or concentrate, the Sun's rays into one intense beam. Solar farms make good use of this idea. The heat they create and channel is used to generate electricity in a variety of ways. In the future, the world's deserts could become the providers of cheap and environmentally-friendly power.

STIRLING ENGINE

A Stirling engine works on the principle that gas expands when heated and contracts when cooled. The Sun's heat is captured and concentrated by mirrors on the engine's cylinder to heat the gas. Inside the closed system of the engine, the heated gas moves between hot and cold cylinders. This moves a piston to turn a crankshaft, which drives the electrical generator.

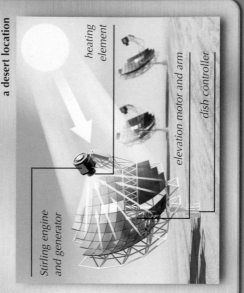

heliostat array in a desert location

heating element

elevation motor and arm

dish controller

Stirling engine and generator

Just 1m² of reflected sunlight provides enough power to run a small electric fire.

Heliostats

These heliostats are made up of 86 one-metre-square mirrors. They are shaped to reflect the sunlight in a concentrated beam on to the heating element of a Stirling engine (*see above*). One Stirling engine can generate enough electricity to power a family home.

Heliostat mirrors, which can be made of any reflective material, are much cheaper to make and maintain than complicated solar, or photoelectric, panels.

> HELIOSTAT – *a system of mirrors that tracks the position of the Sun, concentrating its rays on a fixed point*

A solar plant

The Solar Two plant (below) was built as an experiment in the Mojave desert, USA, where sunshine is guaranteed. The amazing array of mirrors concentrates the Sun's rays and beams them to a receiver at the top of a central tower. The generating equipment, housed on the ground, produces enough electricity to power nearly 3,000 homes.

SUPER SALT

The receiver contains hundreds of small tubes filled with molten salt. The concentrated sunshine heats this to 1,050°C. The salt then moves down to a heat exchanger, where it boils water into steam. The steam drives a turbine to generate electricity, and the salt returns to the top of the tower to be reheated.

heliostats

receiver

hot, molten salt
(inside tank)

turbine generator

turbine

generator

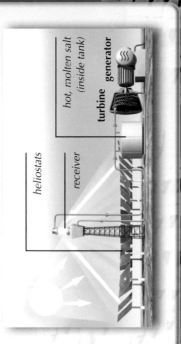

1,926 heliostats cover an area of 82,750m², or almost 20 football pitches.

Large tank stores hot salt before it flows to the heat exchanger.

turbine and electricity generator

> The mirrors of a solar furnace can create a temperature of 3,000°C – half as hot as the Sun.

SOLAR SAILING

Scientists are working on a craft that will be powered by nothing but sunlight. Particles radiating from the Sun put a tiny, tiny amount of pressure on anything they reach – and this is enough, in the vacuum of space, to move an object. A spacecraft with a large enough solar sail to catch the radiation could voyage to the end of the solar system, and beyond, using no fuel at all.

"We can build sails to catch the radiation blowing from the Sun."

Arthur C Clarke (1917–2008)
British science fiction author and inventor

Photons

A beam of sunlight contains uncountable numbers of tiny particles of energy called photons. When sunlight falls on an object, the impact of each photon exerts a minute amount of pressure. Added together, these impulses would push the sail forwards.

NanoSail-D

Scientists at NASA have designed an experimental space sail to help them measure the amount of solar pressure required to move things in space. The sail is made of reflective aluminium foil across a frame of strong, lightweight plastic – but it is far too small to power a spacecraft.

NanoSail-D is 9.3m² in area, weighs only 4.5kg, and can fit into a small suitcase.

> **PHOTON** – *a particle of electromagnetic radiation that moves at the speed of light*

solar-powered Zephyr aircraft (above)

Two-bladed propellers are designed to work high up where the air is very thin.

Lightweight materials amount to only 930kg – about the same weight as a small car.

Solar spy plane

A solar-powered plane is perfect for surveying, mapping or spying on an area. It can fly very high where there's the most sunlight, and because it flies so slowly – about as fast as you can pedal a bicycle – it can fly over one spot for hours or days at a time. This makes it much cheaper than a space satellite.

Solar-powered motors

Fourteen electric motors line the front edge of the giant wing. Each weighs only 5kg, but has the same power as about five bicycles being pedalled. The electricity is fed to each motor by a cable from either the solar cells or the on-board batteries.

NASA's *Helios* aircraft

Helios is the largest and most powerful solar-powered aircraft yet to fly. The flight was only an experiment and the plane carried no crew, but it reached a record height of 30km. Only rockets and rocket-powered planes have gone higher. The top of the huge, 75m-long wing is covered with 62,000 solar cells, which receive light from above and below to maximize their output. Batteries provide back-up power in dark or cloudy conditions.

❯ To propel a one-person spacecraft through space, a solar sail would need to be about 5km² in size.

SATNAV

Without satellites, modern telecommunications and broadcasting would be impossible. Satellites are also used for spying, and to collect data about space and the Earth. One of their most useful jobs, though, is to provide the Global Positioning System (GPS). This has revolutionized navigation. Anybody holding a GPS receiver can know, to the nearest metre, exactly where they are on the surface of the planet.

GPS satellites orbit at a height of about 18,000km.

a hand-held, portable GPS receiver (below)

GPS satellites

Circling around the world are at least 24 GPS satellites, operated by the US Air Force. Each takes 12 hours to orbit (circle) the Earth. The first were launched in 1978 and the GPS system was fully operational by 1995.

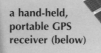

GPS receivers

As long as it can pick up a signal from three satellites, a GPS receiver can fix a position by trilateration (*see panel*). A small computer can then work out the position in latitude and longitude, and even convert it to an exact grid reference on a map.

TRILATERATION – *the process of fixing a point by knowing the distance from three other points*

The latest mobile phones have GPS receivers, so the emergency services know exactly where you are when you call them.

www.sciencemuseum.org.uk/onlinestuff/stories/atomic_clocks.aspx

Automatic navigation

Before radio and GPS, ships' navigators and aircraft pilots had to fix their position using the Sun, stars, lights or landmarks, then work out a route and make regular checks. A satellite navigation ('satnav') system continually fixes position, and uses a computer to calculate the route and make corrections. The software knows where dangers are and plans a course to avoid them.

In-car navigators

Drivers use GPS receivers combined with a computer and a digitalized map system. The software stores data of road maps and routes. The GPS location is fed into the computer, which displays the right part of the map.

Receiver knows the position of the car, and its software can give the driver accurate directions.

Atomic clock

GPS satellites each contain the most accurate of time-measuring devices – the atomic clock. This ensures that they are all perfectly synchronized (in time with each other) as they emit their signals.

"Knowing exactly where you are now is more than half the secret of getting somewhere else."

**Captain James Weddell
(1787–1834)**
British naval navigator and explorer

TRILATERATION: FIXING POSITION

Each GPS satellite transmits a tracking signal at exactly the same time. A receiver on the ground picks up the signals and works out the distance of each satellite. It plots the nearest satellite's position on the surface of an imaginary sphere. The same thing happens with the next two satellites, so that three imaginary spheres are created. The spot where all three spheres meet is the true position of the object on the ground that is being tracked.

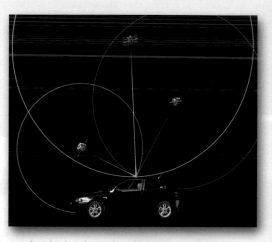

To plot the height of the object, above the ground, a fourth satellite signal is needed.

ECOHOME

Houses such as this one are designed to save energy and be kind to the environment. A typical house built in the 1960s had large windows, very little insulation and central heating that was not carefully controlled. In the 1990s, architects began to plan buildings that used natural energy to the full, created very little waste and did not harm the atmosphere by giving off greenhouse gases.

GREENHOUSE GAS – a gas, such as carbon dioxide, that is present in the Earth's atmosphere and traps heat from the Sun

Solar power

The Sun's rays provide energy that is clean, non-polluting and fairly reliable. They heat and light this house during the day and create extra electricity for it in a row of photoelectric cells or solar panels.

anti-reflective cover glass

contact grid

uncharged silicon

positively-charged silicon

Photoelectric cells consist of two layers of silicon. When sunlight falls on the top layer it makes electrons move down to the bottom layer. This creates electricity.

⊜ ENERGY EFFICIENCY

A house in the 1960s needed a lot of energy to keep it warm because almost 50 per cent of the heat escaped from its walls, windows, floor and roof. A passive house loses nine times less heat through its windows, eight times less through the walls and an amazing 17 times less through the roof. Overall, it is about 11 times more energy efficient.

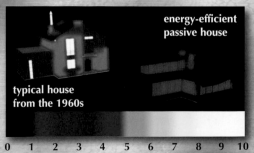

energy-efficient passive house

typical house from the 1960s

0 1 2 3 4 5 6 7 8 9 10

Heat loss is measured in U-values, with zero being the most efficient and ten the least.

Glass has a special coating to reflect heat back into the house.

2–3 layers of glass, with gas in between, protect against heat loss.

Wind turbine

Streamlined vane ensures the turbine always faces the wind.

Turbine with 1m-long blades can generate up to 300 kilowatts of electricity.

This small turbine, driven by the wind, generates enough electricity to power a kettle and light the whole house. Some of the current is stored in batteries, to be used when there is no wind.

Super insulation

Modern insulation materials stop heat passing through them. If windows are triple-glazed, the walls filled with plastic foam and the roof space lagged with a thick blanket of insulating material, very little heat will be lost.

geothermal heating pipes

25cm gap between the outer and inner walls is filled with expanded polystyrene.

Passive house

A passive house does not actively consume power. This one is built on a site that makes the most use of the Sun for light and warmth. It has super-insulated walls, windows and roof, and is airtight to prevent heat leaking out and cold air sneaking in. Most passive houses only need a wood stove or small heat pump to boost the indoor temperature on the coldest days (*see geothermal heating, below*). The heat pump works in reverse in the summer to cool the house.

www.colorcoat-online.com/blog/index.php/2011/05/17-futuristic-eco-homes/

Living roof

Instead of using tiles or concrete, a green – or 'living' – roof is made of a layer of earth containing growing plants. It keeps the house quiet, helps to control its temperature and the plants also absorb harmful carbon dioxide gas from the air.

underfloor heating system

Pump moves the 'refrigerant liquid' around the system.

100m of plastic pipes, linked to the house, buried 1.5m–2m in the ground.

Geothermal heating

To heat or cool the house, a liquid is pumped through pipes buried in the ground. In winter, the soil is warmer than the liquid and heats it. In summertime, the soil temperature cools the warmer liquid down.

DIGIWORLD

"Mary had a little lamb."

Thomas Edison (1847–1931)
American inventor, speaking the first words ever to be recorded and played back, in 1877

In the late 19th century, the inventor Thomas Edison realized that he could record the shape of sound waves with a needle, by cutting grooves in wax. Recorded sound totally changed the way people listened to music in the early 1900s, and there was a second revolution in the 1980s when recording went digital. These days, sound can be recorded at much higher quality, in much greater quantities and increasingly small formats.

DIGITAL FILE – *a collection of small packets of information stored in a computer's memory*

needle or stylus
on a vinyl record

Analogue recording
The wiggly grooves of a record mimic the form of the original sound wave. The electric needle in the pickup runs through the grooves and creates an electrical wave, which is then converted by the loudspeaker into sounds.

compact
discs (CDs)

Digital recording
In digital recording, the original sound wave is converted into a numerical code. The high part of the wave has the highest number and the low part the lowest. This code is etched on to a disc as a series of dots and dashes.

Binary code

The numbers from sampled sound waves are written in binary code. Binary is a way of writing numbers with just two digits – 0 and 1. For example, the number one is written 001, two is 010 and three 011. This is ideal for digital electronics where switches have only two positions – on and off.

MP3 synchronization

Computer software can convert the tracks on a CD into a file format known as MP3. The MP3 files can then be transferred to an MP3 player or a mobile phone, so that people can listen to them while on the move.

Storing digital files

Digital music files, such as MP3s or MP4s, can be used to store many hours of music in a tiny space. The music files that contain the information are compressed so that they use up less memory on the music player's digital hard drive.

Apple *iPod* entertainment system

Player has software that can read the shrunken files and convert them back to audio files.

⊖ INFORMATION IN A SMALLER SPACE

To get 1,000 hours of recorded sound on the vinyl analogue format, you would need a stack of 1,000 records about 5m high, weighing about 400kg. The same amount of information on CD would make a pile of discs 1.5m high and 20kg in weight. A small, portable MP3 player can hold the same amount of data, but is only 5mm thick and 15g in weight.

vinyl records

CDs

portable MP3 player

ROBOT RESCUE

Robots are often used to do jobs in situations that are too dangerous for people – such as clearing landmines, studying active volcanoes or exploring other planets. It is also possible to build computer-controlled, battlefield robots to carry out military tasks in locations close to an opposing army, or to rescue wounded soldiers without risking other human lives.

Soldier's friend

Robots such as this one are being developed to rescue wounded soldiers lying where it is too dangerous for medics to go. Remotely controlled, its tracks can cross rough ground. Its 'head' contains a camera and sensors for locating the casualty. Jointed arms can pull the soldier from danger along a safe route detected by another set of sensors on its body.

remote-controlled camera

radio antenna or aerial

Tiny tank

This small robot can perform jobs such as spying and bomb disposal. Its tracks carry it over rough ground, sand, snow and through water. It can even climb stairs. An operator controls it by radio from a safe distance.

Tracks are driven by a battery-powered electric motor.

The word *robota* is Czech for 'forced labour'. There are about 1.5 million industrial robots working throughout the world.

UAVs can look over hills or spy on enemies without putting soldiers in danger.

Robot spy planes

Unmanned aerial vehicles (UAVs) are large, radio-controlled planes. Soldiers use them mainly to survey, map or spy on areas from above. UAVs can patrol for hours, very slowly and quietly, studying the ground using sensors and cameras.

Hand-launched UAVs are flown by a pilot sitting at a console, either on the ground or inside a safe bunker many kilometres away.

Small petrol engine drives a propeller at the rear.

Fuel-efficient spy

The engine of a *Predator* uses so little fuel that the UAV can stay in the air for up to 40 hours. The *Predator* is almost the size of a small, piloted aircraft with a wingspan of 15m, a length of 8.2m and a weight of 1 tonne. It has a top speed of 217km/h and usually flies at a height of 7,600m.

www.newscientist.com/topic/robots

NANOBOTS

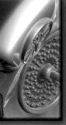

As technology progresses, machines become more powerful. Often, they also become much smaller. The first computers were the size of buses but there is now many, many times more computer power inside a single mobile telephone. Nanotechnology is the science of making working machines so small that you can see them only with a microscope. Nano science is in its infancy, but when it is perfected it will change the world as much as did the discovery of electricity or the invention of computers.

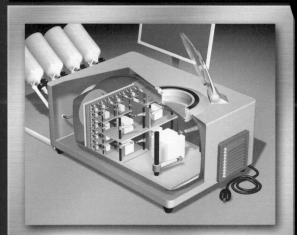

Nanobots may move about by 'swimming' using long legs copied from living bacteria.

Nanobot measures just 0.5–3 microns across.

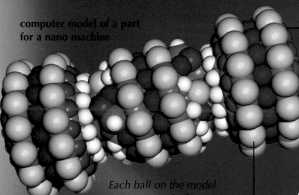

computer model of a part for a nano machine

Each ball on the model represents a single atom.

Molecular construction

Building nano machines involves working with tiny pieces of material made up of individual molecules, each consisting of six or so atoms. The atoms and molecules can be arranged to form tiny components of incredibly small devices.

⊖ NANO FACTORY

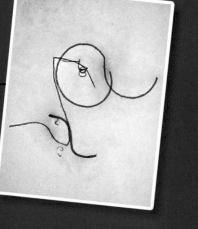

Soon, it might be possible to have a portable 'nano factory', small enough to fit on a desk. Tiny machines inside the device would join together molecules and build them up into larger and larger parts (shown here as white cubes) for use in computers and other electrical equipment.

Tiny tubes

Carbon atoms can be formed into tube-shaped molecules, which are fitted together to form nanotubes. These can be used to conduct an electrical current, or as tiny mechanical parts in a machine. The largest are only 1mm long but they are ten times stronger than steel.

"How I long to have the means to explore the teeming worlds I view through my microscope."

Carl Linnaeus (1707–78)
Swedish scientist

Nanobots in medicine

One day tiny robots, smaller than grains of salt, could be injected into humans and animals to treat diseases. They would carry drugs directly to the cells that needed them or repair damage deep inside veins, arteries and organs. In the distant future, people might have medical nanorobots permanently inside them, checking the body for signs of illness and taking action at once.

**mobile cell repairer
nanorobot (below)**

www.sciencemuseum.org.uk/antenna/nano

chemical sensors for checking and identifying the target cells

manipulating arm with gripper for holding on to individual cells

Tiny claws, chisels and drills would be used to work on diseased tissue.

A tiny computer, inside the nanobot, might be used to navigate around the body.

main probe or manipulator

Machine body made up of carbon molecules and other diamond-like substances.

Injecting cells

In normal drug treatment, large amounts of chemicals are used to make sure the sick cells are reached. This can damage healthy cells and cause side effects. Using a tiny probe, a nanobot would be able to pierce only the diseased cells, injecting just the right amount of the appropriate drug.

red blood cell inside a human artery

The nanobot might use electrodes, high-frequency microwaves or ultrasound to kill off dangerous cancer cells.

Power to operate the nanobot might come from a tiny battery, or a motor powered by the natural glucose and oxygen in the body.

RENDERING – in film and design, this is the process of adding layers and textures to make an object appear realistic

SFX

Film is the only form of art or entertainment that can make the most fantastic and wildest imaginings seem real. Only movies can show battling spaceships, giant waves destroying cities and hordes of evil monsters on the rampage. Such scenes are created using expensive special effects (SFX) that deceive the eye. Film-makers used crude special effects 100 years ago, but a truly realistic appearance has only been possible since the invention of computers.

Blue-screen filming

This is a technique that allows the director to make the actors appear in spectacular or impossible situations. First the actors are filmed in front of a blue or bright green screen. Separately, a background scene is filmed and then, either using computers or special filters, the two pieces of film are joined together so that the actors move realistically in front of the scenery.

The plain green shapes will be rendered by a computer programme, which adds skin and hair textures to make them look lifelike.

**scene from the film
King Kong (2005)**

⊖ SCALE MODELS

Often it is too expensive and difficult to build a full-size setting for a film. Carefully made, highly detailed models stand in as scaled-down versions of the real thing. Clever lighting and computer enhancement make it virtually impossible to notice what is a model and what is real.

This model of a capsized US World War II battleship is about one-third of the actual size.

In the studio
The stars of the film act their part in the studio using props that will be matched and blended into the special effects and live action. This actress (above) is playing her role inside a model to stand in for the giant ape King Kong's thumb and forefinger.

> To make the 2005 version of *King Kong*, $35 million (£23.5 million) was spent on special effects alone.

Actor sits on a marked area that, on film, will become the polar bear's back.

Creature animation

In the past, creature models were animated by filming them frame by frame, re-posing the model slightly in each one. Film-makers now use computer graphics to create natural-looking creatures, which move and behave as if alive.

Virtual lines, joining all the key measuring points on the body, create a 3D grid, or wireframe, of the bear's body (right).

Wireframe technology

After the designers have sketched the creature, an animator creates a virtual body in the form of a flexible 3D grid made up of lots of polygons (shapes). These map out the contours of the body with great accuracy.

First, the actors (below) play the scene in a studio, in front of a blue screen.

When the background is added (above) they appear to be riding in a train through Paris.

"The secret to film is that it's an illusion."

George Lucas (born 1944)

American film director, producer and screenwriter – creator of the Star Wars films

Adding backgrounds

As a background, film or computer-generated images can be joined to the blue-screen footage. Then both sequences are transferred, or rendered, to a computer file. The computer software makes sure all the shadows and lighting match up, and that the two image sequences blend perfectly.

GRAPHIC GAMES

Making the characters in a computer game takes a lot of imagination, skill and enormous amounts of sophisticated computer programming. Thinking of the characters and deciding what they look like comes first. Turning the ideas into an on-screen reality, and making them move around, is more about computer science and mathematics.

Creating the exoskeleton

Once a character is finalized on paper, the animator creates a virtual skeleton for it. This is made up of a 3D grid net, which outlines the body. This external covering, or exoskeleton, is basically a digital version of the jointed, posable wooden figures used by traditional artists.

The surface layer of the exoskeleton is built up gradually.

A polygon mesh, made up of shapes, forms the basic exoskeleton.

Anchor points on the exoskeleton decide the arrangement of the polygon mesh.

Character sketches

Before any computer programming work is done, the characters are developed the old-fashioned way – by drawing. This is the stage for experimenting with all the details and colouring of faces, hairstyles and clothing.

Anchor points

These are the points where parts of the body will revolve, turn or balance to form its key movements. The computer is programmed to know how the joints work, and how heavy the limbs are, so that it can create realistic movements.

Hinges, or avars, are added to the exoskeleton – usually where the body's natural joints would be.

During final rendering, each frame of an animation takes about six hours of computer time to complete.

www.pbs.org/kcts/videogamerevolution/inside/how/02.html

Skin and texture

Once the skeleton has been animated and dressed, the texture of the skin, hair and clothes are finished in detail (rendered) by another software programme. This gives them a more realistic, 3D appearance, rather than a flat, sheetlike surface.

Final rendering

The information that makes up the settings, colours and movements has to be fitted into a single digital file, the equivalent of a single frame in a film. This process is called rendering. Each frame lasts a twenty-fourth of a second. Then, sound effects and music are added.

⊖ CHARACTER ANIMATION

Sometimes, animators employ actors or athletes to wear a special suit and perform all the actions and facial expressions of the character. This suit has sensors called trackers at key points, such as the knees and elbows, which record all the movements. The computer uses this information to create an animation.

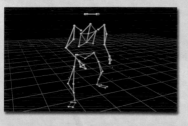

guide wheel

load wheel

track

Coaster wheels

Roller coaster cars have three sets of wheels. Load wheels run on top of the track and carry the weight of the car. Guide wheels run on the sides of the rails and upstop wheels ride under the track. The upstop wheels lock the train to the track and prevent it from flying off.

roller coaster car

Upstop wheels are made of tough steel, with polyurethane tyres.

"Life is like a roller coaster. There are ups and downs, twists and turns... unless you fall off."

Traditional saying

FUN MACHINE

Technology is not just for the serious side of life. It also gives us the roller coaster – a machine good for nothing but thrills, hurling us on a spectacular, stomach-churning ride to nowhere. Pure fun! Roller coasters first appeared in Russia as sleds on icy slides. These became popular in France – but, as France is warmer than Russia, the ice melted. Someone had the idea of fitting wheels to the sleds, and then fitting those wheels on to a track, and so the roller coaster was born.

Centrifugal force

This force overcomes gravity and holds the cars and their passengers on the track as they loop the loop. As the cars accelerate they want to fly off in a straight line, but are forced into the curve by the track. This creates the centrifugal force, which presses and holds the cars against the track.

 > There are almost 2,100 roller coasters operating worldwide.

⊖ FAIRGROUND FORCES

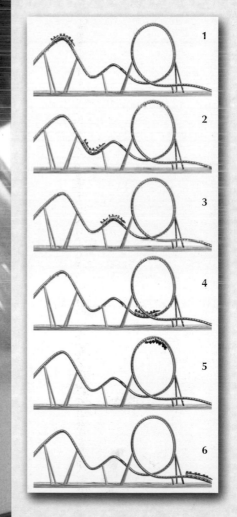

The cars are pulled by a chain to the top of the highest hill (1), and this builds up a lot of potential energy. This turns to kinetic (movement) energy as the cars speed down the first hill (2), and this new momentum carries the cars to the top of the next, smaller hill (3). Dropping down the small hill (4) builds up enough kinetic energy to speed to the top of the loop-the-loop (5), where potential energy builds once again. This transforms, again, into kinetic energy as the cars drop down the other side of the loop (6) and travel on to the next part of the circuit.

World's tallest
This roller coaster towers over the Kingda Ka amusement park in New Jersey, USA. It is 139m to the summit and the cars swoop and corkscrew along its track at 210km/h. The ride itself only lasts for 30 seconds.

GLOSSARY

3D
Three-dimensional – describes an object that has height, width and depth.

acceleration
The act of speeding up or also, in machines, the ability to speed up.

analogue
Describes a device that reproduces data as a continuously changing stream of information, rather than digitally.

atmosphere
The layer of gases that surrounds a planet, such as the Earth.

atom
The smallest particle of a chemical element. An element is a pure substance that is made of only one type of atom.

axle
A rod or spindle that passes through the centre of a wheel, around which the wheel turns.

centrifugal force
A force that acts on something travelling on a circular path, pushing it away from the centre of that circle.

climate
The average weather of a place over a period of time.

crankshaft
An axle (or shaft) that is driven by turning a handle (or crank).

elevon
On the wings of an aircraft, a surface that the pilot can move up or down to adjust the craft's pitch (nose up or nose down) and to stop it from rolling.

fission
The splitting of an atom to release nuclear energy.

gear
A toothed wheel that meshes with other toothed wheels to create a driving force.

generator
A machine that transforms movement energy into electricity.

gravity
The force of attraction between two objects. On Earth, gravity pulls objects towards the centre of the planet and stops them from floating off into space.

hard drive
The part of a computer used for storing digital data.

horsepower
A unit for measuring engine power, based on how much of the same work a horse could do. One unit of horsepower is equal to 750 watts of power.

jack
A device for lifting heavy equipment. Pneumatic jacks are powered by compressed air.

kinetic energy
The extra energy an object has when it is moving.

laser
A device that produces a very thin and powerful beam of light.

microwave
An invisible form of energy, similar to light, used for cooking and communications.

molecule
A group of two or more atoms bonded together.

momentum

The force that an object gathers as it moves, and which keeps it moving.

national grid

A network of power lines within a country that links houses and workplaces with power stations, so that electricity is available to all.

navigation

Finding the way or charting a course.

orbit

The path of one object around another in space.

payload

The cargo carried inside a vehicle.

photoelectric cell

Also called a solar cell. A type of tile, usually made of specially-treated silicon, that collects sunlight and transforms it into electrical energy.

potential energy

The possible energy stored inside an object due to its position (for example, a raised pendulum) or its condition (for example, a charged battery).

ram

A device that puts pressure on something in order to drive it into a particular place.

renewable

Describes a resource or fuel that can be used without it running out for future generations, because it can be replaced naturally or with careful management.

satellite

Anything that goes around, or orbits, something else. Artificial (man-made) satellites travelling around the Earth are used in communications.

sensor

A device that can detect a particular kind of stimulus, such a heat, light, sound or movement.

software

Also known as programmes – the complex instructions used in computer systems, enabling the computer to perform specific functions.

sound wave

The means by which noise travels through air, water or the ground, as a series of vibrations (shaking movements).

stage (of a rocket)

One of the two or more separate sections of a rocket, each of which has its own fuel and engine.

synchronization

Putting things in time with each other.

thrust

The force that pushes something onwards.

turbine

A machine that is used to change movement energy – from flowing water or steam – into a turning motion that powers machinery (such as a generator).

ultrasound

A type of sound wave, outside the range of human hearing, that can be bounced off an unseen object in order to form an image of it.

virtual

Artificially created on a computer.

weightlessness

The experience of being beyond the pull of gravity, such as in space. (Weight is the measurement of how much the force of gravity is acting on an object.)

INDEX

INVESTIGATE

Get in touch with technology by visiting museums and other places of interest – and don't forget to keep up with the news!

Museums and exhibitions

One of the best ways to learn about new technology, and play around with it, is to visit museums and exhibitions near to where you live.

WALL-E (2008) is an animated film set in the future, featuring a lovable waste-collecting robot.

 Wow! Inventions that Changed the World by Philip Ardagh (Macmillan Children's Books/Science Museum)

Launchpad at the Science Museum, Exhibition Road, South Kensington, London SW7 2DD, UK

www.sciencemuseum.org.uk

A child plays with a robot during the *Robot World* exhibition in Taiwan.

Film and fiction

Sometimes, science fiction writers and artists come up with ideas and inventions in books and films, which are later developed and used in real life.

Out Of This World: Science Fiction Stories chosen by Edward Blishen (Kingfisher)

Forbidden Planet (a chain of science fiction stores) 179 Shaftesbury Avenue, London WC2H 8JR, UK

www.disney.co.uk/wall-e/

The president of Panasonic answers questions about his company's state-of-the-art products.

TV and the news

New technology is talked about on TV news bulletins, or in magazine, newspaper and internet articles. So keep your eyes open, or get an adult to save the articles for you!

 BBC *Focus* magazine (monthly science publication)

Newsround (BBC news programme for children)

www.bbc.co.uk/newsround/

A visitor takes photos during an open day at the European Particle Physics Laboratory in Geneva, Switzerland.

Tours and visits

Some industrial plants, power stations and factories – normally closed to the public – offer special tours for schools, or have visitor centres that show you what goes on inside.

Physics: Why Matter Matters! by Dan Green and Basher (Kingfisher)

Sellafield Visitor Centre at Sellafield, Seascale, Cumbria CA20 1PG, UK

www.visitcumbria.com/wc/svc.htm